ENDANGERED!

EAGLES

Karen Haywood

 Marshall Cavendish
Benchmark
New York

Marshall Cavendish Benchmark
99 White Plains Road
Tarrytown, New York 10591
www.marshallcavendish.us

All Web sites were available and accurate when this book was sent to press.

Editor: Karen Ang
Publisher: Michelle Bisson
Art Director: Anahid Hamparian
Series Design by: Elynn Cohen
Cover Design: Kay Petronio

Library of Congress Cataloging-in-Publication Data

Haywood, Karen.
Eagles / by Karen Haywood.
p. cm. -- (Endangered!)
Includes bibliographical references and index.
Summary: "Describes the characteristics, behavior, and plight of
endangered eagle species, and what people can do to help"--Provided by
publisher.
ISBN 978-0-7614-2991-3
1. Eagles--Juvenile literature. 2. Rare birds--Juvenile literature. I. Title.
QL696.F32H39 2009
598.9'42--dc22
2008023375

Front cover: A Philippine eagle
Title page: A white-tailed fish eagle
Back cover: A bald eagle (top); A Philippine eagle (bottom)

Photo research by Pamela Mitsakos
Front cover: Gerry Ellis/Minden Pictures
The photographs in this book are used by permission and through the courtesy of: Photo Researchers, Inc.: Tom McHugh, 32, 34;
J.L.G. Grande, 38, 43. Minden: Neil Lucas, back cover (bottom); Pete Oxford, 14; Tui de Roy, 15. Nature Picture Library: Paul
Hobson, 1; Lynn M. Stone, 6; David Tipling, 12; Patricio Robles Gil, 16; Niall Benvie, 25; Pete Oxford, 26, 28; Nick Garbutt; 31;
Jamme & Jens Eriksen, 36. AP Images: Chris Gardner, 5. Alamy: Ron Niebrugge, 9; Danita Delimont, 20; Mark Bolton
Photography, 41. Animals Animals: Doug Wechsler, 18; Juergen & Christine Sohns, 40. Getty: James P. Blair, 35. Shutterstock:
FloridaStock, back cover (top). Bruce Coleman Inc.: Brian J. Coates, 19. Visuals Unlimited: Fritz Polking, 22.
Printed in China
1 2 3 4 5 6

Contents

Introduction

Eagles are **birds of prey.** This means that they not only hunt for their food, but that they use their feet to catch and hold the food. Eagles have very strong **talons,** or claws. Eagles also have very good eyesight. They can see at least twice as far as any human, perhaps farther. Unlike us, their eyes allow them to see forward and to the side at the same time. These seeing abilities help make the eagles good hunters.

Scientists divide eagles into four groups based on their behaviors or physical characteristics: fish (or sea) eagles, snake (or serpent) eagles, booted (or true) eagles, and harpy (or buteonine) eagles. The first two group names focus on what the eagle eats. Some eagles live near bodies of water and eat fish, while other eagles eat snakes or lizards. The last two group names are based on how the eagle looks. "Booted" eagles have feathers that cover their legs all the way down to their ankles, making them look as though they are wearing boots. Harpy eagles, which are among the largest and strongest birds in the world, are named for a character from mythology. In myths and legends, a harpy had large claws and was especially violent.

Birds have lived on, and flown above, the Earth for millions of years. During that time, the Earth has gone through many natural changes in its environment. Very large, "super" continents have split into new, smaller continents and Ice Ages have come and gone. Through it all, many types of birds have found ways to survive.

However, over the past five hundred years, close to five hundred bird **species,** or types, have not been able to adapt to the changes in their environment—both natural and man-made. As a result, these species have become **extinct.** That is an average of one bird species per year. During this century, *ten* species of birds will disappear each year. Of the fifty-nine species of eagles in the world today, many are in danger of extinction.

Using special bands on the birds' legs or other tracking devices, scientists hope to learn more about endangered eagles and how to protect them.

1

Bald Eagles

The bald eagle has been the national symbol of the United States since 1782. Bald eagles are sea eagles, and they live in regions that cover most of North America, especially near the coasts, large rivers, swamps, and lakes. It is quite a large bird. Females measure about 2 to 3 feet (61 to 91 centimeters) long and weigh up to 15 pounds (6.8 kilograms). Females are slightly larger than males. The **wingspan** of the bald eagle averages around 8 feet (2.4 meters).

A young bald eagle is brown in color, but as it grows older its head and tail feathers slowly turn white. The

Where did this eagle's name come from? Obviously, a bald eagle has feathers on its head and is not bald. When early European colonists described the bird, they used the word balde, *which at that time meant "white," not "hairless."*

bird's beak, claws, and eyes are yellow. All of these colors combine to make a very striking eagle.

One of the bald eagle's preferred food is salmon. It will hunt for these fish by watching from a high perch overlooking a body of water. When it spies a fish swimming below, the eagle takes off and dives toward the surface, snatching up the fish with its mighty talons. The bird then flies high to a perch, where it dines on its catch.

Bald eagles also eat water birds, such as ducks and gulls, and other small animals and reptiles. The eagle may surprise water birds by sneaking up behind a wave in the water and catching them unaware. Other times, it will circle very high above the water or land, choose its target from among the ducks, rabbits, or snakes below, and quickly drop down on it at great speed. This downward dive is called a "stoop."

IN DANGER

When the European settlers first came to this continent, the bald eagle population was in the hundreds of thousands. But as the human population grew, the

For many years, it was rare to find healthy bald eagle chicks in the wild.

number of eagles fell. Settlers cut down forests where the eagles lived and hunted. Humans fished for the same food that the bald eagle needed to survive. The eagle population was in serious trouble by the late 1800s. Many eagles were shot for their feathers or simply for sport. The bird also suffered as a result of eating poisoned food. Farmers and ranchers often left out poisoned bait to kill animals that they thought were attacking their livestock.

Congress eventualy passed the Bald Eagle Protection Act of 1940, which also protected the golden eagle. Unfortunately, around the same time, farmers began to use DDT. This **pesticide** got into the lakes and rivers, poisoning the fish that the eagles ate, which caused female eagles to lay eggs with very thin shells. When they tried to sit on their eggs to keep them warm, the shells broke and the baby eagles would not grow and hatch.

As the situation grew more serious in the 1960s and early 1970s, many states put the bald eagle on their lists of endangered species. The national Endangered Species Act was signed into law in 1973. Around the same time, the use of DDT was made illegal in the United States. In 1976, the U.S. Fish and Wildlife Service formally listed the bald eagle as a national endangered species.

In the following years, **conservation** efforts were made to protect the eagles. Special land was set aside where animals—including the eagles—were allowed to live free and untouched by humans. Scientists and conservationists also bred the eagles in captivity. Eagles bred in captivity are hatched and raised somewhere safe—such as at a wildlife preserve or in a zoo—and then released into the wild. The hope is that these released eagles will stay healthy and boost wild eagle populations. Increased knowledge about bald eagle habits and what was going wrong also helped people to protect and increase the bald eagle population.

By 1995, the bald eagle was no longer considered endangered because the population of these birds in the lower forty-eight states (not including Alaska or Hawaii) had grown from fewer than 300 in 1963, to more than 9,000 in 1994. The bald eagle was then formally classified as **threatened,** or at a risk of becoming endangered.

Thanks to strict laws and concerned citizens, the bald eagles' recovery was so successful that in 2007, the U.S. Fish and Wildlife Service removed the bald eagle from the federal list of threatened species. Bald eagles will continue to be covered by the Bald and Golden Eagle Protection Act (BGEPA) and the Migratory Bird Treaty Act (MBTA). Both laws protect bald eagles by prohibiting killing, selling, or otherwise harming the eagles, their nests, or their eggs.

However, **habitat** destruction still remains an issue. Scientists are concerned that the bald eagle population may still decline in the next thirty to forty years. More people are building houses near the water, which is the bald eagle's preferred habitat. The eagles, since they are sea eagles, need large areas of its waterfront habitat. By setting aside more of this land as national parks and sanctuaries, these eagles will have a better chance of living in the wild.

2

Harpy Eagles

The harpy eagle's **range** covers the regions in southeastern Mexico to northern Argentina and southern Brazil. This bird's habitat is the tropical lowland rain forests found there. These eagles usually prefer to nest in the silk-cotton, or kapok, trees. These trees are about 131 feet (40 m) off the ground. A harpy eagle nest normally measures about 5 feet (1.5 m) wide.

The harpy eagle is a fascinating looking bird. It is the largest of all eagles, and probably the most powerful bird of prey. A harpy eagle has a wingspan that can be 8 feet (2.4 m). Its talons can be the size of grizzly bear claws! Female harpies are often twice the size and twice the

These birds probably got their name from the harpies of ancient Greek mythology. Those harpies were scary creatures—part-woman and part-bird with deadly claws.

Harpy eagle claws are very large and can be very deadly.

weight of males. Females may grow to be 3.3 feet (1 m) tall and can weigh up to 20 pounds (9 kg).

Harpy eagles eat animals that live in the trees of the rain forest. They hunt sloths, monkeys, opossums, iguanas, rodents, and birds. These birds are truly eagle-eyed and can see something as small as 1 in (2.54 cm) long from almost 220 yards (200 m) away. They dive down to their prey and snatch it with their massive talons. To help spot its next meal, the harpy eagle can turn its head upside down to get a better look!

DECREASING NUMBERS

The harpy eagle is endangered. They were often hunted for their feathers, as prizes, or because people thought

Like the creatures in mythology, a harpy eagle can be violent when it is defending its nest or attacking prey.

they were dangerous. As with too many other birds and animals, habitat destruction is also threatening the eagles' survival. The rain forests are being cut down for wood products and to make space for farms, ranches, and other human settlements.

There are some conservation efforts going on in Panama at the Soberania National Park and La Amistad International Park, and in Belize at Chiquibul Forest. For this beautiful and powerful bird to survive, laws against hunting it must be passed and new national parks and sanctuaries must be created for them.

3

Philippine Eagles

The Philippine eagle used to be called the monkey-eating eagle, because it was one of the only eagles big enough to catch and eat monkeys. It originally inhabited the rain forests and mountains of Luzon, Samar, Leyte, and Mindanao, which are islands in the Philippines.

The harpy eagle is the only eagle larger than the Philippine eagle, but the Philippine eagle is still a very powerful bird of prey. This eagle's back is covered in brown feathers, its chest and face are white and brown. It is the only bird of prey with blue eyes. The top of its head has a crest of feathers that can stick out. The Philippine

Wild Philippine eagles are only found on some of the islands in the Philippines.

The rainforests of the Philippines are the perfect habitat for these tropical birds.

eagle's bill, or beak, is black and is fiercely hooked at the tip. This helps it catch and eat its prey. The Philippine eagle's legs and feet are yellow with long, dark talons. Female Philippine eagles can weigh up to 15.5 pounds (7 kg) and measure between 2.8 to 3.5 feet (86 to 102 cm) in length. Philippine eagles have large wings, and a 6-foot (1.8-meter) wingspan.

These eagles have a varied diet. They rely on rain forest animals, which include eight species of mammals, four species of snakes and reptiles, and three species of

The eagle's sharp claws hold the prey still while its beak tears into the meal.

other birds. Although they are called monkey-eating, monkeys make up only 3 percent of the eagles' diet. Flying lemurs—which are related to monkeys— make up 54 percent of the Philippine eagle's diet.

ENDANGERED

Since the 1960s, the Philippine eagle has been on the verge of extinction. This is mostly because of the **deforestation** of its habitat. Before the 1940s, the islands

To make space for farms and other human communities, rain forest in the Philippines are cut down or burned.

of the Philippines were covered in tropical rain forests—each island was more than 80 percent rain forest. But much of the forest was cut down for lumber and to make space for human communities. By the 1990s, rain forests covered only 20 percent of most of those islands. Without the forests and the animals that live there, the eagles have no home and no source of food.

Today, it is estimated that there are only 500 Philippine eagles left in the wild. The Philippine Eagle Foundation is working hard to save this national bird and its environment. They hope to accomplish this by educating farmers about using the land wisely and by encouraging them to plant native fruit trees. These fruit trees may help the farmers make more money, while also preserving the natural plant and animal life of the Philippines. Special wildlife centers also take care of Philippine eagles. They rescue sick or injured eagles with the hopes of releasing the birds back into the wild. These centers also breed Philippine eagles to be released into the wild. Understanding what these birds need and preserving the rainforests will help to save this national symbol.

4

White-Tailed Sea Eagles

The white-tailed sea eagle is the fourth-largest eagle in the world. This eagle lives in Greenland, Europe, and parts of Asia. Most of its feathers are brown, except for its lighter-colored head and its tail, which is white. Its eyes, beak, and talons are bright yellow. It can grow to 3 feet (just under 1 m) tall with a wingspan of up to 8 feet (2.5 m). This bird prefers to live along the seacoasts, the valleys of large rivers, and around inland lakes, near their favorite food—fish. They will also eat other birds—especially ducks

The white-tailed eagle gets its name from the distinctive coloring on its tail.

and other waterfowl—mammals, and a large amount of carrion, which are the remains of dead animals. Most of the eagle's time is spent perched perfectly still in trees, waiting to spot its prey. This is known as still hunting.

AT RISK

White-tailed eagles were often shot by farmers who thought the birds killed their livestock. As a result, white-tailed eagles became extinct in Great Britain in the early 1900s. In Sweden, some of these birds are still shot every year. People also steal their eggs.

White-tailed eagles also die from eating food poisoned by pollution, especially the chemical mercury. This chemical is leaked from factories or from garbage. Mercury causes the birds to suffer from weight loss, weak wings, and weak legs. This leads to difficulty flying, walking, and perching. Water contaminated by mercury is a serious problem today for many species of birds and animals.

Despite a serious effort to reintroduce the white-tailed eagle to Scotland, where it had become extinct in the early 1900s, the numbers are still very low. A new plan called Mull Eagle Watch has been started to help protect eagle nests and their eggs.

In March 2007, the European Commission (a governing body made up of people from different European nations) accused Poland of violating European environmental law. The Polish government had planned to build a highway through the Rospuda Valley in northeastern Poland. This

Stopping the unnecessary killing of these birds and preserving wild habitats is the only way that these eagles will survive.

area of Poland is protected by Europe's major environmental protection laws. One of the many threatened and endangered animals that lives there is the white-tailed sea eagle. Construction of the highway in most of that region has been halted while a decision is being made. In the meantime, conservationists around the world are trying to educate the public about how to protect these eagles.

5

Madagascar Eagles

There are two kinds of very rare eagles that live only on the island of Madagascar. Madagascar is located in the Indian Ocean off the southeastern coast of Africa. It is one of the largest islands in the world. Madagascar is considered one of the world's top ten wildlife conservation concerns because of the many species that live only on the island. However, many native species are disappearing as a result of human interference and habitat loss. Both of the Madagascar eagles were added to the endangered species list in 1995.

The Madagascar fish eagle is one of the several endangered animal species that live only in Madagascar.

A Madagascar fish eagle calls out for its mate from high in a tree.

MADAGASCAR FISH EAGLE

This eagle, the largest raptor in Madagascar, is one of the rarest birds of prey. It lives along the west coast of the island, from Morombe in the southwest to Diego Suarez in the north. The Madagascar fish eagle prefers forests near lakes and rivers, but it can also be found in swamps and along rocky coasts. In order to build their nests and hunt, they need large trees or cliffs close to the water. This eagle eats mainly fish and crabs.

The Madagascar fish eagle has dark reddish-brown feathers on most of its body, except for its white cheeks, throat, and its short tail. It is 23 to 25 inches (58 to 64 cm) long, with a wingspan of about 6.5 feet (2 m). This eagle is close to extinction because people have drained wetlands and cleared forests in order to farm. As a result, the bird has lost much of its natural habitat and has nowhere to live or hunt. To make matters worse, mining work has polluted many of Madagascar's rivers. Fewer fish can live in the rivers, and those that do are not easily spotted by the eagles through the dirty water.

However, good news for this eagle came in January 2007, when the government of Madagascar granted legal protection to the Mahavavy-Kinkony Wetlands for two years. This area holds all of the wetland bird species found in western Madagascar. Many of them, like the Madagascar fish eagle, which has a population of only 220 birds, are found nowhere else on Earth. Many people hope that this protection will last for more than two years and that the eagles will have a chance to increase their numbers.

MADAGASCAR SERPENT EAGLE

Until it was rediscovered in 1993, the Madagascar

serpent eagle was thought to be extinct. It now can be found in eastern areas of the island, but especially in the Masoala National Park. This is a very secretive eagle. It does not venture far beyond the edge of the lowland tropical rain forest where it prefers to live. In fact, scientists who study this kind of eagle often have a hard time finding them. As a result, there are very few photographs of these eagles in the wild.

This is a medium-sized eagle that is a little over 2 feet (66 cm) tall. Its feathers are brown on its head and back, and it has stripes of brown and white on its chest. This serpent eagle has a tail longer than most eagles, with black and brown stripes. Like many other eagles, it has long, powerful, yellow legs and talons.

The Madagascar serpent eagle eats lizards, especially chameleons and leaf-tailed geckos. It will hunt on the ground as well as from the air.

The rain forest habitat of this eagle is being destroyed for farming and for logging. Other threats include fires that destroy the forests and poor mining practices that

A river that runs through the forests in Masoala National Park is an ideal habitat for the Madagascar serpent eagles.

pollute the land and water. Since this species depends on untouched rain forest, it may become extinct again.

The good news is that the species has been found recently in several protected areas—national parks and reserves, and in one protected forest. The Madagascar serpent eagle is the subject of an ongoing research program in the Masoala National Park, and scientists hope to find out more about the eagle and how to protect it.

6

Pallas's Fish Eagles

Pallas's fish eagle is also called Pallas's sea eagle, but it is rarely found near the sea. It prefers the wetlands in parts of Asia and India. Some of these eagles can be found around large lakes, swamps, and rivers in Mongolia, China, and northern India.

Pallas's fish eagle is a large bird. It is mostly dark brown, but its head, neck, and throat are pale brown. Its blackish-colored tail has a broad white band. This eagle is

This eagle is probably named after Peter Simon Pallas, a German scientist who lived during the eighteenth century.

Pallas's fish eagles will also eat small land animals, such as frogs and rodents.

about 2.5 to 2.75 feet (76 to 84 cm) tall. Its wingspan ranges between 6 and 7 feet (180 to 205 cm) and it weighs between 4.5 and 8 pounds (2 to 3.7 kg).

As its name suggests, this eagle's diet is mainly made up of fish. It prefers to capture them at the water's surface rather than diving under water for them. The eagle will also eat frogs, turtles, reptiles, waterfowl, and other birds. What it eats, however, depends on the region. It may eat nothing but frogs and turtles in one place, or nothing but waterfowl that swim on a fish-less lake in the Punjab Salt Range of Pakistan.

Protected wetlands in Keoladeo National Park in India provide homes for many different birds—including endangered Pallas's fish eagles.

Its view from the sky allows this fish eagle to see its prey beneath the water, and then efficiently swoop down for the catch.

IN DANGER

Because wetlands have been drained and trees cut down for agriculture and property development, the Pallas's fish eagle is at risk. The sources for food and the places to nest are disappearing. Another problem is the pollution of water with pesticides and waste from factories and other businesses. The development of oil and gas fields is a threat in parts of Asia. Oil and gas fields destroy native environments and the waste products hurt the local animals. In China, hunting is a problem because the eagle's tail feathers are a valuable collector's item.

For this eagle to survive, the wetlands they call home must be protected and set aside so that human development cannot destroy them. Also, more public awareness programs must be available. These programs would teach people about their native wildlife and how they can peacefully live alongside these animals. Preserving the land and the wildlife on it is healthier for everyone—humans and animals alike.

7

Spanish Imperial Eagles

The Spanish imperial eagle is one of the rarest and most threatened birds of prey in the world. This eagle has a pale brown head and neck, but dark brown feathers on the rest of its large, powerful body. There is a white area on the shoulders, which explains why it is sometimes called the white-shouldered eagle. An average female eagle is about 2.5 to 2.75 feet (75 to 84 cm) tall. It can weigh up to 7.7 pounds (3.5 kg). As with most eagles, the male Spanish imperial eagle is smaller.

The Spanish imperial eagle is also known as the white-shouldered eagle or Adalbert's eagle.

Like most eagles, the Spanish imperial eagle has very good eyesight that helps it catch its prey.

This eagle prefers to live in the cork oak forests, plains, and hills of central Spain.

Spanish law forbids the cutting or digging out of cork and other similar trees. Only when the trees are dead or diseased is permission given to remove the tree. Still, it is said that the cork trees are sometimes removed or cut illegally to make way for more valuable crops or real estate development. This is just one of the problems the eagles face.

Nests can be found high up in the branches of these trees in a small Spanish forest.

The Spanish imperial eagle also likes the flood plains, dunes, savannas, and high mountain slopes where there is no irrigated farmland. The fact that most of Spain has been turned into farmland is very bad news for this eagle. The development of many types of farms is an ongoing problem. An increase in tourism also affects the region. As more people come to visit, more land is developed to make way for stores and other businesses. While tourism helps the economy and the people living in the area, too much tourism hurts the land and the native animals.

The main item in the Spanish imperial eagle's diet is rabbit, although in the winter this eagle is known to eat wild geese. Both the eagle and its prey depend on their homes in the forests and other wilderness areas.

IN DANGER

In the 1960s, only thirty pairs of this eagle remained in Spain. Since 1987, national and regional governments have passed many conservation laws. These efforts succeeded in increasing the population of the Spanish imperial eagle by a large amount. Since 1994, though, the population has declined to fewer than 200 pairs. Researchers believe that many eagles are being electrocuted on power lines. Between 1991 and 1999, however, around 14,000 dangerous electric towers were changed to make them less dangerous to birds. This has helped to reduce deaths from electrocution.

The Spanish imperial eagle needs what one scientist called "emergency care units" where the birds can be protected and saved from extinction. People who work at

Without government protection, wild Spanish imperial eagles will not be able to reproduce and create future generations.

these units would provide the eagles a safe place to stay, treat any serious injuries, and provide food. One such place is the Doñana National Park in southwestern Spain. Unfortunately, one reserve cannot provide food for many eagles. If they are to survive, these large birds need more protected habitats and a larger supply of food.

GLOSSARY

birds of prey—Birds that hunt and kill smaller animals for food. These are also called raptors.

conservation—A careful preservation and protection of something, such as an animal or habitat.

deforestation—The action or process of clearing an area of forests.

endangered—Any species that is in danger of extinction throughout all or a significant portion of its range

extinct—No longer existing.

habitat—The place or type of place where a plant or animal naturally or normally lives or grows.

pesticide—A substance used to destroy pests, such as insects or other small animals.

prey—Animals that are hunted and used as food.

range—The place where a certain kind of animal or plant naturally lives.

species—A specific type of animal. For example, bald eagles are a species of eagle.

talon—The claw of an animal—especially of a bird of prey.

threatened—In the case of animals, to be at risk of becoming endangered.

wingspan—The distance from the tip of one wing to the tip of the other wing.

FIND OUT MORE

Books

Gunzi, Christiane. *The Best Book of Endangered and Extinct Animals*. New York: Kingfisher, 2004.

Hickman, Pamela. *Birds of Prey Rescue: Changing the Future for Endangered Wildlife*. Richmond Hill, Ontario: Firefly Books, 2006.

Nobleman, Marc Tyler. *Eagles*. New York: Marshall Cavendish Benchmark, 2007.

Richardson, Adele D. *Eagles: Birds of Prey*. Mankato, MN: Bridgestone Books, 2002.

Web Sites

Carolina Raptor Center
http://www.carolinaraptorcenter.org

Eagle Cam—U.S. Fish & Wildlife Service
http://www.fws.gov/nctc/cam/eaglecam.htm

Eagles—PBS Nature
http://www.pbs.org/wnet/nature/eagles

Kids' Planet—Defenders of Wildlife
http://www.kidsplanet.org

ORGANIZATIONS

Defenders of Wildlife
1130 17th Street, NW
Washington, DC 20036
http://www.defenders.org

National Audubon Society
700 Broadway
New York, NY 10003
http://www.audubon.org

The Nature Conservancy
Worldwide Office
4245 North Fairfax Drive, Suite 100
Arlington, VA 22203-1606
http://www.nature.org

World Wildlife Fund
U.S. Headquarters
1250 Twenty-Fourth Street, N.W.
PO Box 97180
Washington, DC 20090-7180
http://www.worldwildlife.org

ABOUT THE AUTHOR

Karen Haywood has edited and written many books for young readers. She lives in North Carolina where she watches the squirrels steal fruit from the apple trees in her backyard as she writes. Inspired by the first Earth Day in 1970, she has been a strong advocate for the environment and animal rights for many years.

INDEX

Page numbers in **boldface** are illustrations.